Great Works

Instructional Guides for Literature

A Wrinkle in Time

A guide for the novel by Madeleine L'Engle
Great Works Author: Emily R. Smith

SHELL EDUCATION

Publishing Credits

Robin Erickson, *Production Director*; Lee Aucoin, *Creative Director*; Timothy J. Bradley, *Illustration Manager*; Emily R. Smith, M.A.Ed., *Editorial Director*; Amber Goff, *Editorial Assistant*; Don Tran, *Production Supervisor*; Corinne Burton, M.A.Ed., *Publisher*

Image Credits

Cover image justdd/Ewa Studio/Shutterstock

Standards

© 2007 Teachers of English to Speakers of Other Languages, Inc. (TESOL)
© 2007 Board of Regents of the University of Wisconsin System. World-Class Instructional Design and Assessment (WIDA).
© Copyright 2010. National Governors Association Center for Best Practices and Council of Chief State School Officers. All rights reserved

Shell Education

5301 Oceanus Drive
Huntington Beach, CA 92649-1030
http://www.shelleducation.com
ISBN 978-1-4258-8990-6
© 2014 Shell Educational Publishing, Inc.

Table of Contents

How to Use This Literature Guide

Today's standards demand rigor and relevance in the reading of complex texts. The units in this series guide teachers in a rich and deep exploration of worthwhile works of literature for classroom study. The most rigorous instruction can also be interesting and engaging!

Many current strategies for effective literacy instruction have been incorporated into these instructional guides for literature. Throughout the units, text-dependent questions are used to determine comprehension of the book as well as student interpretation of the vocabulary words. The books chosen for the series are complex and exemplars of carefully crafted works of literature. Close reading is used throughout the units to guide students toward revisiting the text and using textual evidence to respond to prompts orally and in writing. Students must analyze the story elements in multiple assignments for each section of the book. All of these strategies work together to rigorously guide students through their study of literature.

The next few pages will make clear how to use this guide for a purposeful and meaningful literature study. Each section of this guide is set up in the same way to make it easier for you to implement the instruction in your classroom.

Theme Thoughts

The great works of literature used throughout this series have important themes that have been relevant to people for many years. Many of the themes will be discussed during the various sections of this instructional guide. However, it would also benefit students to have independent time to think about the key themes of the novel.

Before students begin reading, have them complete *Pre-Reading Theme Thoughts* (page 13). This graphic organizer will allow students to think about the themes outside the context of the story. They'll have the opportunity to evaluate statements based on important themes and defend their opinions. Be sure to have students keep their papers for comparison to the *Post-Reading Theme Thoughts* (page 64). This graphic organizer is similar to the pre-reading activity. However, this time, students will be answering the questions from the point of view of one of the characters of the novel. They have to think about how the character would feel about each statement and defend their thoughts. To conclude the activity, have students compare what they thought about the themes before the novel to what the characters discovered during the story.

How to Use This Literature Guide *(cont.)*

Vocabulary

Each teacher overview page has definitions and sentences about how key vocabulary words are used in the section. These words should be introduced and discussed with students. There are two student vocabulary activity pages in each section. On the first page, students are asked to define the ten words chosen by the author of this unit. On the second page in most sections, each student will select at least eight words that he or she finds interesting or difficult. For each section, choose one of these pages for your students to complete. With either assignment, you may want to have students get into pairs to discuss the meanings of the words. Allow students to use reference guides to define the words. Monitor students to make sure the definitions they have found are accurate and relate to how the words are used in the text.

On some of the vocabulary student pages, students are asked to answer text-related questions about the vocabulary words. The following question stems will help you create your own vocabulary questions if you'd like to extend the discussion.

- How does this word describe _____'s character?
- In what ways does this word relate to the problem in this story?
- How does this word help you understand the setting?
- In what ways is this word related to the story's solution?
- Describe how this word supports the novel's theme of . . . .
- What visual images does this word bring to your mind?
- For what reasons might the author have chosen to use this particular word?

At times, more work with the words will help students understand their meanings. The following quick vocabulary activities are a good way to further study the words.

- Have students practice their vocabulary and writing skills by creating sentences and/or paragraphs in which multiple vocabulary words are used correctly and with evidence of understanding.
- Students can play vocabulary concentration. Students make a set of cards with the words and a separate set of cards with the definitions. Then, students lay the cards out on the table and play concentration. The goal of the game is to match vocabulary words with their definitions.
- Students can create word journal entries about the words. Students choose words they think are important and then describe why they think each word is important within the book.

How to Use This Literature Guide *(cont.)*

Analyzing the Literature

After students have read each section, hold small-group or whole-class discussions. Questions are written at two levels of complexity to allow you to decide which questions best meet the needs of your students. The Level 1 questions are typically less abstract than the Level 2 questions. Level 1 is indicated by a square, while Level 2 is indicated by a triangle.

These questions focus on the various story elements, such as character, setting, and plot. Student pages are provided if you want to assign these questions for individual student work before your group discussion. Be sure to add further questions as your students discuss what they've read. For each question, a few key points are provided for your reference as you discuss the novel with students.

Reader Response

In today's classrooms, there are often great readers who are below average writers. So much time and energy is spent in classrooms getting students to read on grade level, that little time is left to focus on writing skills. To help teachers include more writing in their daily literacy instruction, each section of this guide has a literature-based reader response prompt. Each of the three genres of writing is used in the reader responses within this guide: narrative, informative/explanatory, and opinion/argument. Students have a choice between two prompts for each reader response. One response requires students to make connections between the reading and their own lives. The other prompt requires students to determine text-to-text connections or connections within the text.

Close Reading the Literature

Within each section, students are asked to closely reread a short section of text. Since some versions of the novels have different page numbers, the selections are described by chapter and location, along with quotations to guide the readers. After each close reading, there are text-dependent questions to be answered by students.

Encourage students to read each question one at a time and then go back to the text and discover the answer. Work with students to ensure that they use the text to determine their answers rather than making unsupported inferences. Once students have answered the questions, discuss what they discovered. Suggested answers are provided in the answer key.

How to Use This Literature Guide *(cont.)*

Close Reading the Literature *(cont.)*

The generic, open-ended stems below can be used to write your own text-dependent questions if you would like to give students more practice.

- Give evidence from the text to support . . . .
- Justify your thinking using text evidence about . . . .
- Find evidence to support your conclusions about . . . .
- What text evidence helps the reader understand . . . ?
- Use the book to tell why _____ happens.
- Based on events in the story, ...
- Use text evidence to describe why . . . .

Making Connections

The activities in this section help students make cross-curricular connections to writing, mathematics, science, social studies, or the fine arts. In some of these lessons, students are asked to use the author as a mentor. The writing in the novel models a skill for them that they can then try to emulate. Students may also be asked to look for examples of language conventions within the novel. Each of these types of activities requires higher-order thinking skills from students.

Creating with the Story Elements

It is important to spend time discussing the common story elements in literature. Understanding the characters, setting, and plot can increase students' comprehension and appreciation of the story. If teachers discuss these elements daily, students will more likely internalize the concepts and look for the elements in their independent reading. Another very important reason for focusing on the story elements is that students will be better writers if they think about how the stories they read are constructed.

Students are given three options for working with the story elements. They are asked to create something related to the characters, setting, or plot of the novel. Students are given choice on this activity so that they can decide to complete the activity that most appeals to them. Different multiple intelligences are used so that the activities are diverse and interesting to all students.

How to Use This Literature Guide (cont.)

Culminating Activity

This open-ended, cross-curricular activity requires higher-order thinking and allows for a creative product. Students will enjoy getting the chance to share what they have discovered through reading the novel. Be sure to allow them enough time to complete the activity at school or home.

Comprehension Assessment

The questions in this section are modeled after current standardized tests to help students analyze what they've read and prepare for tests they may see in their classrooms. The questions are dependent on the text and require critical-thinking skills to answer.

Response to Literature

The final post-reading activity is an essay based on the text that also requires further research by students. This is a great way to extend this book into other curricular areas. A suggested rubric is provided for teacher reference.

Correlation to the Standards

Shell Education is committed to producing educational materials that are research and standards based. In this effort, we have correlated all of our products to the academic standards of all 50 United States, the District of Columbia, the Department of Defense Dependents Schools, and all Canadian provinces.

Purpose and Intent of Standards

Standards are designed to focus instruction and guide adoption of curricula. Standards are statements that describe the criteria necessary for students to meet specific academic goals. They define the knowledge, skills, and content students should acquire at each level. Standards are also used to develop standardized tests to evaluate students' academic progress. Teachers are required to demonstrate how their lessons meet standards. Standards are used in the development of all of our products, so educators can be assured they meet high academic standards.

How To Find Standards Correlations

To print a customized correlation report of this product for your state, visit our website at http://www.shelleducation.com and follow the online directions. If you require assistance in printing correlation reports, please contact Customer Service at 1-877-777-3450.

Correlation to the Standards (cont.)

Standards Correlation Chart

The lessons in this guide were written to support the Common Core College and Career Readiness Anchor Standards. This chart indicates which sections of this guide address the anchor standards.

Common Core College and Career Readiness Anchor Standard	Section
CCSS.ELA-Literacy.CCRA.R.1—Read closely to determine what the text says explicitly and to make logical inferences from it; cite specific textual evidence when writing or speaking to support conclusions drawn from the text.	Close Reading the Literature Sections 1–5; Comprehension Assessment
CCSS.ELA-Literacy.CCRA.R.2—Determine central ideas or themes of a text and analyze their development; summarize the key supporting details and ideas.	Theme Thoughts; Analyzing the Literature Sections 1–5; Creating with the Story Elements Sections 1–5
CCSS.ELA-Literacy.CCRA.R.3—Analyze how and why individuals, events, or ideas develop and interact over the course of a text.	Close Reading the Literature Sections 1–5; Analyzing the Literature Sections 1–5; Reader Response Sections 1–5; Creating with the Story Elements Sections 1–5
CCSS.ELA-Literacy.CCRA.R.4—Interpret words and phrases as they are used in a text, including determining technical, connotative, and figurative meanings, and analyze how specific word choices shape meaning or tone.	Vocabulary Sections 1–5
CCSS.ELA-Literacy.CCRA.R.5—Analyze the structure of texts, including how specific sentences, paragraphs, and larger portions of the text (e.g., a section, a chapter) relate to each other and the whole.	Analyzing the Literature Sections 1–5
CCSS.ELA-Literacy.CCRA.R.10—Read and comprehend complex literary and informational texts independently and proficiently.	Entire Unit
CCSS.ELA-Literacy.CCRA.W.1—Write arguments to support claims in an analysis of substantive topics or texts using valid reasoning and relevant and sufficient evidence.	Analyzing the Literature Sections 1–5; Reader Response Sections 1–5; Close Reading the Literature Sections 1–5; Post-Reading Response to Literature

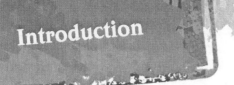

Correlation to the Standards (cont.)

Standards Correlation Chart (cont.)

Common Core College and Career Readiness Anchor Standard	Section
CCSS.ELA-Literacy.CCRA.W.2—Write informative/explanatory texts to examine and convey complex ideas and information clearly and accurately through the effective selection, organization, and analysis of content.	Reader Response Sections 2–3, 5; Post-Reading Response to Literature
CCSS.ELA-Literacy.CCRA.W.3—Write narratives to develop real or imagined experiences or events using effective technique, well-chosen details and well-structured event sequences.	Reader Response Sections 1, 4–5
CCSS.ELA-Literacy.CCRA.W.4—Produce clear and coherent writing in which the development, organization, and style are appropriate to task, purpose, and audience.	Close Reading the Literature Sections 1–5; Analyzing the Literature Sections 1–5; Reader Response Sections 1–5; Post-Reading Response to Literature
CCSS.ELA-Literacy.CCRA.L.4—Determine or clarify the meaning of unknown and multiple-meaning words and phrases by using context clues, analyzing meaningful word parts, and consulting general and specialized reference materials, as appropriate.	Vocabulary Sections 1–5
CCSS.ELA-Literacy.CCRA.L.6—Acquire and use accurately a range of general academic and domain-specific words and phrases sufficient for reading, writing, speaking, and listening at the college and career readiness level; demonstrate independence in gathering vocabulary knowledge when encountering an unknown term important to comprehension or expression.	Vocabulary Sections 1–5

TESOL and WIDA Standards

The lessons in this book promote English language development for English language learners. The following TESOL and WIDA English Language Development Standards are addressed through the activities in this book:

- **Standard 1:** English language learners communicate for social and instructional purposes within the school setting.

- **Standard 2:** English language learners communicate information, ideas and concepts necessary for academic success in the content area of language arts.

About the Author—Madeleine L'Engle

Madeleine L'Engle Camp was born on November 29, 1918. Her early years were spent in New York City. When she was in elementary school, she liked writing for fun rather than doing her schoolwork. She enjoyed writing poems and stories. She started keeping a journal when she was only eight years old.

When she was 12 years old, she moved from New York to the French Alps. She attended an English boarding school in the Alps, where she continued her passion for writing. In 1933, her family returned to the United States, and she attended a boarding school in South Carolina for high school. From 1937–1941, L'Engle attended Smith College in Massachusetts. There she studied what she loved, and her love for writing helped her to be very successful in her studies. She graduated with honors.

Once she graduated, L'Engle returned to live in a part of New York City called Greenwich Village. Living and working in this creative community gave her the freedom to write. She published two novels in these important years after graduating from college. Her first two books were called *A Small Rain* and *Ilsa*.

She married Hugh Franklin and had a daughter. She settled with her new family in Connecticut and continued to write. Eventually, her family returned to New York City, and L'Engle continued to write as her children grew up. It was during this time that L'Engle wrote *A Wrinkle in Time*, her most famous book. *A Wrinkle in Time* was rejected many times before it was published in 1962 and subsequently won the Newbery Award.

Much of her adult life was spent as a volunteer librarian at the Cathedral of St. John the Divine in New York City. Her books reflect her interest in science as well as her Christian faith. At times, her books have been controversial because of her religious views and how they are reflected in her books.

L'Engle toured throughout the world speaking about her books. During her life, she encouraged children to read and write during their free time. She passed away on September 6, 2007.

Be sure to check out her website: http://www.madeleinelengle.com/

Possible Texts for Text Comparisons

There are four other books in L'Engle's science-fiction series: *A Wind in the Door*, *A Swiftly Tilting Planet*, *Many Waters*, and *An Acceptable Time*. *A Ring of Endless Light* or *Troubling a Star* may also be used for enriching text comparisons by the same author.

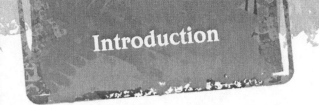

Book Summary of *A Wrinkle in Time*

Meg Murry is a unique girl in her town. No one except her younger brother Charles Wallace really seems to understand her. She is very close to both her mother and father, but even they cannot make her understand what is so special about her and why she's so different from everyone else.

Meg's father has disappeared. This makes her feel even more separated from her peers. Then, some very unlikely characters find their way into Meg's life. Three peculiar women take Meg, Charles Wallace, and Meg's new friend, Calvin, on a mysterious adventure. They *tesser* through time and space to new planets.

The group learns about the Black Thing, which has been threatening the universe for many years. Although good forces have been fighting this evil for a long time, it still manages to control certain planets in the solar system. This includes the planet where Mr. Murry is being held, Camazotz. Eventually, the group ends up on Camazotz, a very strange planet where IT and his minion, the man with red eyes, control everything.

At that point, the problem in the story gets compounded. Not only is Meg looking for her missing father, but now Meg must try to save her brother from IT's control. Meg finds her father, and together they try to fight IT and get Charles Wallace back to normal. Unfortunately, IT is just too powerful. Meg, Calvin, and Mr. Murry have to tesser off of Camazotz without Charles Wallace.

While under the care of some very strange creatures on a planet called Ixchel, Meg realizes that she is the only one who can save her brother. She must return to Camazotz alone and use her greatest strengths to save Charles Wallace. Meg does not completely understand how she has any strengths that could beat IT, but she returns to Camazotz anyway to try. When she is fighting IT's power once more, she suddenly realizes that her ability to love and be loved is something that only she has. IT has no love. This knowledge is what helps Meg focus her love on her brother and thereby save him from evil.

Cross-Curricular Connection

This book can be used during a science unit on space.

Possible Texts for Text Sets

- Collins, Suzanne. *Gregor the Overlander*. Scholastic, 2004.
- Greathouse, Lisa. *The Wonder of Our Solar System*. Teacher Created Materials, 2007.
- Hollingsworth, Tamara. *Neil Armstrong: Man on the Moon*. Teacher Created Materials, 2010.
- Jankowski, Connie. *The Wonder of Outer Space*. Teacher Created Materials, 2008.
- Wells, H.G. *The Time Machine*. W.W. Norton & Co., 2008.

Name _____

Date _____

Pre-Reading Theme Thoughts

Directions: Read each of the statements in the first column. Decide if you agree or disagree with the statements. Record your opinion by marking an X in Agree or Disagree for each statement. Explain your choices in the third column. There are no right or wrong answers.

Statement	Agree	Disagree	Explain Your Answer
Good should always win over evil.			
Your physical appearance is not very important in society.			
Love is stronger than hatred.			
Individual differences are crucial to a society.			

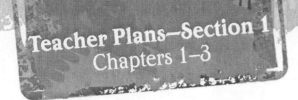
Vocabulary Overview

Ten key words from this section are provided below with definitions and sentences about how the words are used in the book. Choose one of the vocabulary activity sheets (pages 15 or 16) for students to complete as they read this section. Monitor students as they work to ensure the definitions they have found are accurate and relate to the text. Finally, discuss these important vocabulary words with students. If you think these words or other words in the section warrant more time devoted to them, there are suggestions in the introduction for other vocabulary activities (page 5).

Word	Definition	Sentence about Text
vulnerable (ch. 1)	someone who is easily hurt or wounded	Charles Wallace looks **vulnerable** in the kitchen in the middle of the night.
prodigious (ch. 1)	tremendous, amazing, exceptional	Mrs. Murry refers to Charles Wallace's word of the day as **prodigious**.
sullen (ch. 1)	bad-tempered, gloomy, moody	Meg feels **sullen** when she compares herself to her mother.
indignantly (ch. 1)	in an offended or mad tone	Various characters use an **indignant** tone when they speak.
tesseract (ch. 1)	a wrinkle in time, the fifth dimension, a way to travel through space and time	Mrs Whatsit says that **tesseracts** exist, and that shocks Mrs. Murry.
warily (ch. 2)	with caution or concern	Meg looks at the principal **warily** when he talks about her father.
antagonistic (ch. 2)	hostile, unfriendly, hard to get along with	The principal calls Meg **antagonistic**.
dilapidated (ch. 2)	falling down, in disrepair	The Mrs Ws are staying in a **dilapidated** old house.
assimilate (ch. 2)	absorb, ingest, take in	Charles Wallace **assimilates** information about Mrs Who.
tangible (ch. 3)	touchable, real, solid	The descriptive word **tangible** is used in similes throughout the book.

Name _____

Date _____

Understanding Vocabulary Words

Directions: The following words are in this section of the book. Use context clues and reference materials to determine an accurate definition for each word.

Word	Definition
vulnerable (ch. 1)	
prodigious (ch. 1)	
sullen (ch. 1)	
indignantly (ch. 1)	
tesseract (ch. 1)	
warily (ch. 2)	
antagonistic (ch. 2)	
dilapidated (ch. 2)	
assimilate (ch. 2)	
tangible (ch. 3)	

Name _____

Date _____

During-Reading Vocabulary Activity

Directions: As you read these chapters, record at least eight important words on the lines below. Try to find interesting, difficult, intriguing, special, or funny words. Your words can be long or short. They can be hard or easy to spell. After each word, use context clues in the text and reference materials to define the word.

- _____
- _____
- _____
- _____
- _____
- _____
- _____
- _____
- _____
- _____

Directions: Respond to the questions about these words in this section.

1. How does the word **sullen** describe Meg Murry's character?

   _____

   _____

2. In what ways does Charles Wallace seem **prodigious**?

   _____

   _____

Analyzing the Literature

Provided below are discussion questions you can use in small groups, with the whole class, or for written assignments. Each question is given at two levels so you can choose the right question for each group of students. Activity sheets with these questions are provided (pages 18–19) if you want students to write their responses. For each question, a few key discussion points are provided for your reference.

Story Element	■ Level 1	▲ Level 2	Key Discussion Points
Character	Describe Meg or Charles Wallace.	Compare and contrast either Meg or Charles Wallace with yourself.	When discussing Charles Wallace and/or Meg, students need to mention their intelligence and their difficulty fitting into society. These two aspects of their characters are pivotal to the understanding of their roles in this book.
Setting	In what ways does this story seem possible?	Discuss in what ways this story fits the genre of science fiction.	This book fits the genre of science fiction because time travel or traveling through dimensions seems like something that could happen with new technologies in the future.
Character	Who is Calvin and why is he important?	In what ways do you think Calvin will play an important role in this story?	Calvin adds a very personal side to Meg's character. He gives the reader a perspective of Meg other than her view of herself. This is important when it comes to trying to save Mr. Murry.
Plot	What is the problem in this story?	Describe how the problem in the story may relate to tesseracts.	Mrs. Murry's reaction to the word *tesseract* is important. Even though the reader doesn't know what a tesseract is yet, you realize it must have something to do with Mr. Murry's disappearance and his choices as a scientist.

Name _____

Date _____

◼ Analyzing the Literature

Directions: Think about the section you have just read. Read each question and state your response with textual evidence.

1. Describe Meg or Charles Wallace.

_____

_____

_____

_____

2. In what ways does this story seem possible?

_____

_____

_____

_____

3. Who is Calvin and why is he important?

_____

_____

_____

_____

4. What is the problem in this story?

_____

_____

_____

_____

▲ Analyzing the Literature

Directions: Think about the section you have just read. Read each question and state your response with textual evidence.

1. Compare and contrast either Meg or Charles Wallace with yourself.

_____

_____

_____

_____

2. Discuss in what ways this story fits the genre of science fiction.

_____

_____

_____

_____

3. In what ways do you think Calvin will play an important role in this story?

_____

_____

_____

_____

4. Describe how the problem in the story may relate to tesseracts.

_____

_____

_____

_____

Name _____

Date _____

Reader Response

Directions: Choose one of the following prompts about this section to answer. Be sure you include a topic sentence in your response, use textual evidence to support your opinion, and provide a strong conclusion that summarizes your opinion.

Writing Prompts

- **Narrative Piece**—Meg is very smart, but she is not a good student in school. Describe any challenges you face in school.
- **Opinion/Argument Piece**—What do you learn about the Mrs Ws that you think will be important later in the novel?

_____

_____

_____

_____

_____

_____

_____

_____

_____

_____

_____

_____

_____

_____

Name _____

Date _____

Close Reading the Literature

Directions: Closely reread the section in chapter 1 in which Mrs Whatsit visits the Murrys. Start when she enters the kitchen, "After a few moments . . ." and continue until she leaves, "The door slammed." Read each question and then revisit the text to find the evidence that supports your answer.

1. In what ways are the Murrys surprised during Mrs Whatsit's visit?

   _____

   _____

   _____

2. Give evidence from the text to describe Charles Wallace.

   _____

   _____

   _____

   _____

3. Use the book to tell how Meg feels about Mrs Whatsit during this visit.

   _____

   _____

   _____

   _____

4. Based on this scene, what role do you think Mrs Whatsit will have in this book?

   _____

   _____

   _____

   _____

Name _____

Date _____

Making Connections—Soap vs. Oil

Mr. and Mrs. Murry are scientists. In fact, they even conduct experiments in their own home. Have you ever conducted a science experiment at home? Below is an easy experiment that you can do in your own kitchen, or even in your classroom.

Have you ever wondered why environmentalists use dish soap to clean animals after an oil spill? Or, maybe you've thought about how soap works when you are doing the dishes at home. You may know that using soap is better than just washing something with water. The soap helps to cut through the grease and dirt and makes it easier to wash away the grime. Try this experiment to see how soap surrounds oil.

Materials

- two jars with tight tops
- water
- food coloring
- cooking oil
- dish soap
- measuring cups
- measuring spoons

Procedure

1. Put a cup of water in each jar. Add 2 drops of food coloring to each jar. Lightly shake the jars.

2. Add one-half cup of oil to each jar. (The oil, food coloring, and water are the same in each jar, so they are constants in the experiment.)

3. Add a small amount of dish soap to one of the jars. (This is the variable.)

4. Tightly put the lids on the jars, and shake both of the jars.

Response

1. What happens inside each of the jars?

   _____

   _____

   _____

2. For what reasons do you think the reactions in the two jars are different?

   _____

   _____

   _____

   _____

   _____

Name _____

Date _____

Creating with the Story Elements

Directions: Thinking about the story elements of character, setting, and plot in a novel is very important to understanding what is happening and why. Complete **one** of the following activities about what you've read so far. Be creative and have fun!

Characters

Draw a picture of what you think Charles Wallace's or Meg's room looks like. Include details that are specific to the character. At the bottom of the picture, write a creative name for your picture that reflects the character's personality.

Setting

Create a map of the setting so far in the book. Your map should include the Murry house, the dilapidated house of the Mrs Ws, Meg's school, and the apple orchard. Be sure that your map is detailed. Label the map clearly so that others know what you've created.

Plot

Create a visual storyboard that shows what major events have happened so far. (If you'd prefer, you can create a written flow chart instead.) Don't include the minor details. For these three chapters, you should probably have about five to seven events.

Vocabulary Overview

Ten key words from this section are provided below with definitions and sentences about how the words are used in the book. Choose one of the vocabulary activity sheets (pages 25 or 26) for students to complete as they read this section. Monitor students as they work to ensure the definitions they have found are accurate and relate to the text. Finally, discuss these important vocabulary words with students. If you think these words or other words in the section warrant more time devoted to them, there are suggestions in the introduction for other vocabulary activities (page 5).

Word	Definition	Sentence about Text
corporeal (ch. 4)	describes something that has a physical form	When you tesser, your **corporeal** body vanishes.
axis (ch. 4)	the center around which something rotates	Earth spins around its **axis**.
inexorable (ch. 4)	stubborn, can't be stopped	As Meg comes out of the first tesseract, she feels in tune with the earth including the **inexorable** tug of the moon.
ineffable (ch. 4)	strange and difficult to define	The **ineffable** quality of the beautiful location helps Meg calm down after her first tesser experience.
ephemeral (ch. 4)	lasting a short time	Meg describes Mrs Which's costume broomstick as **ephemeral** since it disappears quickly.
virtue (ch. 4)	being morally good	Even as a winged creature, Meg knows that Mrs Whatsit has **virtue**.
metamorphose (ch. 4)	change completely	Mrs Whatsit **metamorphoses** into a beautiful flying creature.
monoliths (ch. 4)	huge tall stones	Meg sees great **monoliths** while flying on the back of Mrs Whatsit.
protoplasm (ch. 5)	the living part of a cell	When Mrs Which lands on the two-dimensional planet, she forgets that the children's **protoplasm** is three-dimensional.
cosmos (ch. 5)	everything that exists anywhere	The fight against the Black Thing is being fought throughout the **cosmos**.

Name _____

Date _____

Understanding Vocabulary Words

Directions: The following words are in this section of the book. Use context clues and reference materials to determine an accurate definition for each word.

Word	Definition
corporeal (ch. 4)	
axis (ch. 4)	
inexorable (ch. 4)	
ineffable (ch. 4)	
ephemeral (ch. 4)	
virtue (ch. 4)	
metamorphose (ch. 4)	
monoliths (ch. 4)	
protoplasm (ch. 5)	
cosmos (ch. 5)	

Name _____

Date _____

During-Reading Vocabulary Activity

Directions: As you read these chapters, record at least eight important words on the lines below. Try to find interesting, difficult, intriguing, special, or funny words. Your words can be long or short. They can be hard or easy to spell. After each word, use context clues in the text and reference materials to define the word.

- _____
- _____
- _____
- _____
- _____
- _____
- _____
- _____
- _____

Directions: Respond to the questions about these words in this section.

1. How does the word **ineffable** relate to describing a tesseract?

   _____

   _____

2. Describe what you think Mrs Whatsit's true **corporeal** state might look like.

   _____

   _____

Analyzing the Literature

Provided below are discussion questions you can use in small groups, with the whole class, or for written assignments. Each question is given at two levels so you can choose the right question for each group of students. Activity sheets with these questions are provided (pages 28–29) if you want students to write their responses. For each question, a few key discussion points are provided for your reference.

Story Element	■ Level 1	▲ Level 2	Key Discussion Points
Plot	What is the black thing that Mrs Whatsit shows the children on Uriel?	Describe how the characters feel about the black thing that they see with Mrs Whatsit on Uriel.	Without knowing why, the characters know that the dark shadow is evil. Meg describes how she feels as "fear that was beyond shuddering, beyond crying or screaming, beyond the possibility of comfort."
Plot	In what dimension is a tesseract?	In what ways does a tesseract relate to geometry and the dimensions?	A tesseract is in the fifth dimension. This is a good time to talk about the three dimensions they already know and then the fourth and fifth dimensions that are introduced in this book.
Character	How does Charles Wallace react when he sees the black thing surrounding Earth?	Describe some other humans throughout time who may have been "fighters" from Earth.	Charles Wallace passionately hates the Black Thing, however he is also the first one to realize who a fighter might have been. As long as students can defend their choices, they should be able to name anyone in history who was a "light," or fighter of the Black Thing.
Setting	Describe the locations to which the children tesser during this section.	In what ways are the different planets important to what is occurring in this book?	The first planet, Uriel, is very beautiful and safe. It is the perfect first stop on this scary adventure through time and space. The second planet is only two dimensions, so the humans suffer. The third planet, in Orion's belt, is gray and colorless. It's important that the characters and readers realize how diverse life can be throughout space.

Name _____

Date _____

Analyzing the Literature

Directions: Think about the section you have just read. Read each question and state your response with textual evidence.

1. What is the black thing that Mrs Whatsit shows the children on Uriel?

   _____

   _____

   _____

   _____

2. In what dimension is a tesseract?

   _____

   _____

   _____

   _____

3. How does Charles Wallace react when he sees the black thing surrounding Earth?

   _____

   _____

   _____

   _____

4. Describe the locations to which the children tesser during this section.

   _____

   _____

   _____

   _____

Name _____

Date _____

Name _____

Date _____

Name _____

Date _____

Reader Response

Directions: Choose one of the following prompts about this section to answer. Be sure you include a topic sentence in your response, use textual evidence to support your opinion, and provide a strong conclusion that summarizes your opinion.

Writing Prompts

- **Opinion/Argument Piece**—Brave men and women have fought the black thing throughout time. Choose someone you know personally and defend why that person could be a "fighter."
- **Informative/Explanatory Piece**—Describe what it means to tesser in your own words.

_____

_____

_____

_____

_____

_____

_____

_____

_____

_____

_____

_____

_____

Name _____

Date _____

Close Reading the Literature

Directions: Closely reread approximately the first three pages of Chapter 4. You can stop reading when Charles Wallace hugs Meg and Meg asks where she is. Read each question, and then revisit the text to find the evidence that supports your answer.

1. Describe what Meg feels the first time she travels by "wrinkling" through time.

    _____

    _____

    _____

2. Calvin says, "Well, just give me time, will you? I'm older than you are." What does he mean by this?

    _____

    _____

    _____

3. Use text evidence to describe the ways that the characters are protective of each other.

    _____

    _____

    _____

4. Based on the events in this section of the story, what do you think will happen next?

    _____

    _____

    _____

Name _____

Date _____

Making Connections–Geometry's Dimensions

Directions: The concept of the fifth dimension is very difficult for Meg to understand. When you were younger, you may have had a similar difficulty understanding the first, second, and third dimensions. Let's revisit that information now. Follow these steps to put Meg into different dimensions.

1. Think about what Meg would look like in zero dimensions. If you realize that she'd be just a point, you're on the right track. Impossible, right?

2. In one dimension, she'd just be a line. Still impossible!

3. Now, add another dimension to Meg. How about we use length and height? Draw Meg in two dimensions. Cut out your two-dimensional Meg. Move Meg around in a two-dimensional world. She can't stand up off your desk! That would be a tough life.

4. Let's see if we can add another dimension to Meg. You need to give Meg some width. Figure out a way to make your two-dimensional Meg stand up. Once you do that, you've created a three-dimensional character.

5. Start over. Create a new Meg that is three-dimensional. However, instead of just adding something to make her stand up, add width for her whole body so that your whole character is three-dimensional.

6. How could you show a fourth dimension for your new Meg character?

    _____

    _____

    _____

    _____

Follow-up Activity: When you have time, read *Flatland* by Edwin A. Abbott. This book depicts a world that is only in two dimensions.

Name _____

Date _____

Creating with the Story Elements

Directions: Thinking about the story elements of character, setting, and plot in a novel is very important to understanding what is happening and why. Complete **one** of the following activities about what you've read so far. Be creative and have fun!

Characters

Draw a picture of the three children riding on the back of Mrs Whatsit as they fly over Uriel. In your picture, include details for the characters as well as the planet that they are on.

Setting

Create a poster advertising life on Uriel. The poster should give at least five reasons why people might want to move to the planet. Be creative with your reasons! Make sure your poster is big, bold, and beautiful.

Plot

Take two of the characters out of this story and put them into another story that has a dark, menacing enemy. Then, write a conversation that might happen between the characters. For example, Meg and Calvin could suddenly be in the middle of Hogwarts with Harry Potter. The three characters can all talk about how they are going to fight Voldemort. If you prefer, you can create your conversation as a comic strip with speech bubbles.

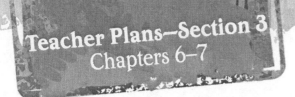

Vocabulary Overview

Ten key words from this section are provided below with definitions and sentences about how the words are used in the book. Choose one of the vocabulary activity sheets (pages 35 or 36) for students to complete as they read this section. Monitor students as they work to ensure the definitions they have found are accurate and relate to the text. Finally, discuss these important vocabulary words with students. If you think these words or other words in the section warrant more time devoted to them, there are suggestions in the introduction for other vocabulary activities (page 5).

Word	Definition	Descriptive Sentence
writhe (ch. 6)	to twist or squirm, sudden turning motion	The Happy Medium shows the Black Thing **writhe** as it surrounds Earth's lightness.
solidify (ch. 6)	becoming more solid	As the Happy Medium shows images to the children, the visions **solidify** and can be seen more clearly.
precipitously (ch. 6)	suddenly, abruptly	Meg thinks they were taken **precipitously** from their apple orchard at the beginning of the book.
propitious (ch. 6)	favorable, likely to be successful	Mrs Whatsit tells the children to wait for the **propitious** moment to try to save their father.
talisman (ch. 6)	a lucky charm that protects you	Mrs Whatsit gives each child a reminder of his or her personal **talisman** when she must leave the children alone on Camazotz.
resilience (ch. 6)	ability to recover quickly	Charles Wallace's gift from Mrs Whatsit as they arrive on Camazotz is his **resilience** because he's still a child.
aberration (ch. 6)	not normal or typical	The woman in the house on Camazotz says there hasn't been a child who was an **aberration** in their section for years.
bilious (ch. 7)	sickly shade of green	The green marble in the CENTRAL Central Intelligence building reflects on people's faces and makes them look **bilious**.
remote (ch. 7)	far away, distant	As the children approach the man with red eyes, Charles Wallace's voice becomes **remote**.
obliquely (ch. 7)	not done directly	Meg tries to look **obliquely** at the man with red eyes so she won't be hypnotized.

Name _____

Date _____

Understanding Vocabulary Words

Directions: The following words are in this section of the book. Use context clues and reference materials to determine an accurate definition for each word.

Word	Definition
writhe (ch. 6)	
solidify (ch. 6)	
precipitously (ch. 6)	
propitious (ch. 6)	
talisman (ch. 6)	
resilience (ch. 6)	
aberration (ch. 6)	
bilious (ch. 7)	
remote (ch. 7)	
obliquely (ch. 7)	

Name _____

Date _____

During-Reading Vocabulary Activity

Directions: As you read these chapters, record at least eight important words on the lines below. Try to find interesting, difficult, intriguing, special, or funny words. Your words can be long or short. They can be hard or easy to spell. After each word, use context clues in the text and reference materials to define the word.

- _____

- _____

- _____

- _____

- _____

- _____

- _____

- _____

- _____

- _____

Directions: Now, organize your words. Rewrite each of your words on a sticky note. Work as a group to create a bar graph of your words. You should stack any words that are the same on top of one another. Different words appear in different columns. Finally, discuss with your teacher why certain words were chosen more often than other words.

Analyzing the Literature

Provided below are discussion questions you can use in small groups, with the whole class, or for written assignments. Each question is given at two levels so you can choose the right question for each group of students. Activity sheets with these questions are provided (pages 38–39) if you want students to write their responses. For each question, a few key discussion points are provided for your reference.

Story Element	■ Level 1	▲ Level 2	Key Discussion Points
Character	Describe what we learn about Mrs Whatsit's past life.	In what ways does being a star prepare Mrs Whatsit for her challenge with the Murry children?	Mrs Whatsit was a star who lost her star life fighting the Black Thing. This experience gives her a lot of motivation to help the Murry children rescue their father and fight against the evil.
Character	What do we learn about Calvin's home life in this section?	Describe how Calvin's relationship with his mother differs from the Murry children's relationships with their mother.	We learn that Calvin's mother is abusive to her children. Although distracted by her missing husband, Mrs. Murry loves her children and cares for them the best that she can.
Setting	What is your first impression of Camazotz?	What strange things do you notice right away about Camazotz?	The new planet feels very comfortable to Meg at first look. Only the behavior of the three Mrs Ws makes the children wary. The fact that the Camazotz children play and the mothers behave in rhythm with one another is very bizarre.
Plot	The man with red eyes seems very interested in Charles Wallace. Why?	For what reasons does the man with red eyes want Charles Wallace to look into his eyes?	From the first chapter, we've known there is something special about Charles Wallace. He seems able to read the minds of people around him. This otherworldly quality may be what the man with red eyes desires.

Name _____

Date _____

Analyzing the Literature

Directions: Think about the section you have just read. Read each question and state your response with textual evidence.

1. Describe what we learn about Mrs Whatsit's past life.

_____

_____

_____

_____

2. What do we learn about Calvin's home life in this section?

_____

_____

_____

_____

3. What is your first impression of Camazotz?

_____

_____

_____

_____

4. The man with red eyes seems very interested in Charles Wallace. Why?

_____

_____

_____

_____

Name _____

Date _____

▲ Analyzing the Literature

Directions: Think about the section you have just read. Read each question and state your response with textual evidence.

1. In what ways does being a star prepare Mrs Whatsit for her challenge with the Murry children?

   _____

   _____

   _____

   _____

2. Describe how Calvin's relationship with his mother differs from the Murry children's relationships with their mother.

   _____

   _____

   _____

   _____

3. What strange things do you notice right away about Camazotz?

   _____

   _____

   _____

4. For what reasons does the man with red eyes want Charles Wallace to look into his eyes?

   _____

   _____

   _____

   _____

Name _____

Date _____

Reader Response

Directions: Choose one of the following prompts about this section to answer. Be sure you include a topic sentence in your response, use textual evidence to support your opinion, and provide a strong conclusion that summarizes your opinion.

Writing Prompts

- **Informative/Explanatory Piece**—Describe why you would or would not want to live like the people on Camazotz.
- **Opinion/Argument Piece**—What advice do you think the Mrs Ws would give to Meg after she realizes that Charles Wallace is "gone"?

_____

_____

_____

_____

_____

_____

_____

_____

_____

_____

_____

_____

_____

_____

Name _____

Date _____

Close Reading the Literature

Directions: Closely reread the end of chapter 7. Begin when Charles Wallace sits down to try the food provided by the man with red eyes. Stop reading at the end of chapter 7. Read each question, and then revisit the text to find the evidence that supports your answer.

1. In what ways does Charles Wallace have a different reaction to the food than Calvin and Meg do?

   _____

   _____

   _____

2. Use the book to explain what the man with red eyes means by "come in and find out what I am."

   _____

   _____

   _____

   _____

3. Based on the events in the book until this point, why does Charles Wallace believe that he has to try to trust the man with red eyes?

   _____

   _____

   _____

   _____

4. Describe what Meg means when she says, "That isn't Charles! Charles is gone!"

   _____

   _____

   _____

Name _____

Date _____

Making Connections– Writing Questions about Time Travel

Directions: Wouldn't it be amazing to travel through time? Create a list of questions or thinking prompts using the following stems. These thinking prompts must relate to the idea of time travel. You should think about how time travel might affect your life, the country, the world, and even future generations.

Stem to Use	Your Question or Thinking Prompt
What . . . ?	
How . . . ?	
Why . . . ?	
I wonder if . . .	
Predict . . .	

Hopefully, you can see that your questions or thinking prompts got more complex as you wrote each one. Now, it's time to choose one to respond to in at least one paragraph. Use the lines below and/or more paper to give a complete response to your favorite prompt.

_____

_____

_____

_____

_____

_____

Name _____

Date _____

Creating with the Story Elements

Directions: Thinking about the story elements of character, setting, and plot in a novel is very important to understanding what is happening and why. Complete **one** of the following activities about what you've read so far. Be creative and have fun!

Characters

Choose Meg or Calvin. Create a Venn diagram for the character. On one side, draw small images or list words for all of the positive qualities of the character's personality. On the other side, draw small images or list words for all of the negative qualities of the character's personality. In the middle, include anything that both helps and hurts the character during the story.

Setting

Draw a picture or make a diorama of what Camazotz looks like when the children first arrive. Your scene should include the street with children playing and mothers in the houses. Include many details to make your image interesting.

Plot

Without looking ahead, write the next one to two pages in the book. What will happen next? Make sure you try to mimic Madeleine L'Engle's style and vocabulary!

Vocabulary Overview

Ten key words from this section are provided below with definitions and sentences about how the words are used in the book. Choose one of the vocabulary activity sheets (pages 45 or 46) for students to complete as they read this section. Monitor students as they work to ensure the definitions they have found are accurate and relate to the text. Finally, discuss these important vocabulary words with students. If you think these words or other words in the section warrant more time devoted to them, there are suggestions in the introduction for other vocabulary activities (page 5).

Word	Definition	Descriptive Sentence
pinioned (ch. 8)	bound, restrained	Meg tries to attack the man with red eyes and she ends up with her arms **pinioned** behind her back by his guards.
wryly (ch. 8)	in an ironic or grim way	Calvin **wryly** says thanks to the man with red eyes after he tells the guards to release them.
swivet (ch. 8)	panic	Calvin feels that he is in a **swivet** during their time talking to the man with red eyes.
pedantic (ch. 8)	someone who knows many small facts and details	As Charles Wallace talks about Camazotz, his voice sounds like the **pedantic** voice of Meg's principal, Mr. Jenkins.
ominous (ch. 8)	threatening or foreboding	While walking with Charles Wallace, Meg begins to feel that the room they enter is **ominous**.
emanate (ch. 8)	to give out or emit	At times, Charles Wallace **emanates** disapproval toward Meg and Calvin.
deviate (ch. 8)	turn away from the expected course	People on Camazotz are not allowed to **deviate** from others.
implored (ch. 9)	desperately begged	Meg **implores** her father to help Charles Wallace.
omnipotent (ch. 9)	someone who can do anything	During this book, Meg comes to realize that her father is not **omnipotent**.
miasma (ch. 9)	a cloud of smelly gas	A red **miasma** surrounds Meg every time she starts to give in to IT's power.

Name _____

Date _____

Understanding Vocabulary Words

Directions: The following words are in this section of the book. Use context clues and reference materials to determine an accurate definition for each word.

Word	Definition
pinioned (ch. 8)	
wryly (ch. 8)	
swivet (ch. 8)	
pedantic (ch. 8)	
ominous (ch. 8)	
emanate (ch. 8)	
deviate (ch. 8)	
implored (ch. 9)	
omnipotent (ch. 9)	
miasma (ch. 9)	

Name _____

Date _____

During-Reading Vocabulary Activity

Directions: As you read these chapters, record at least eight important words on the lines below. Try to find interesting, difficult, intriguing, special, or funny words. Your words can be long or short. They can be hard or easy to spell. After each word, use context clues in the text and reference materials to define the word.

- _____
- _____
- _____
- _____
- _____
- _____
- _____
- _____
- _____
- _____

Directions: Respond to the questions about these words in this section.

1. How is the word **deviate** important to the leaders of Camazotz?

_____

_____

2. In what ways does the word **ominous** describe CENTRAL Central Intelligence?

_____

_____

Analyzing the Literature

Provided below are discussion questions you can use in small groups, with the whole class, or for written assignments. Each question is given at two levels so you can choose the right question for each group of students. Activity sheets with these questions are provided (pages 48–49) if you want students to write their responses. For each question, a few key discussion points are provided for your reference.

Story Element	■ Level 1	▲ Level 2	Key Discussion Points
Setting	List at least two things that do not exist on Camazotz that exist on Earth.	Compare and contrast your life on Earth with the lives of the people who live on Camazotz.	Freedom should be a major difference that students point out. They could also include life, liberty, and the pursuit of happiness. People on Earth can be individual and independent. There is little synchronization on Earth on a day-to-day basis.
Character	Meg calls out to Mrs Whatsit, asking for help. Why doesn't Mrs Whatsit come to help the children?	Describe the reasons that the three Mrs Ws cannot go to Camazotz and do not come to help the children once Charles Wallace is under IT's control.	At this point in the book, the reasons that the Mrs Ws cannot go to Camazotz are not completely clear. However, the fact seems pretty clear that Meg and Charles Wallace have to conquer this evil on their own. They can have outside help, but they have to face the evil on their own and overcome it. It's almost like there are rules for this adventure that they're on.
Character	Meg doesn't like being different from her peers. Why is it important to allow people to be unique?	What are the dangers in having a society where no one is allowed to be different?	Students will have very different opinions here. Allow them to talk about their own lives and how they feel the same as or different from their peers.
Plot	Why is IT so dangerous to Meg?	For what reasons is Charles Wallace trying to get Meg under IT's control?	If Meg falls under IT's control, there won't be anyone to save Charles Wallace. For reasons that are not completely clear yet, Meg is the only one who is able to save him, and he needs to be saved. The controlled part of Charles Wallace knows that he needs Meg on his side to get more powerful.

Name _____

Date _____

Analyzing the Literature

Directions: Think about the section you have just read. Read each question and state your response with textual evidence.

1. List at least two things that do not exist on Camazotz that exist on Earth.

   _____

   _____

   _____

2. Meg calls out to Mrs Whatsit, asking for help. Why doesn't Mrs Whatsit come to help the children?

   _____

   _____

   _____

3. Meg doesn't like being different from her peers. Why is it important to allow people to be unique?

   _____

   _____

   _____

4. Why is IT so dangerous to Meg?

   _____

   _____

   _____

   _____

Name _____

Date _____

▲ Analyzing the Literature

Directions: Think about the section you have just read. Read each question and state your response with textual evidence.

1. Compare and contrast your life on Earth with the lives of the people who live on Camazotz.

_____

_____

_____

2. Describe the reasons that the three Mrs Ws cannot go to Camazotz and do not come to help the children once Charles Wallace is under IT's control.

_____

_____

_____

_____

3. What are the dangers in having a society where no one is allowed to be different?

_____

_____

_____

_____

4. For what reasons is Charles Wallace trying to get Meg under IT's control?

_____

_____

_____

_____

Name _____

Date _____

Reader Response

Directions: Choose one of the following prompts about this section to answer. Be sure you include a topic sentence in your response, use textual evidence to support your opinion, and provide a strong conclusion that summarizes your opinion.

Writing Prompts

- **Opinion/Argument Piece**—What qualities does Meg have that you think you should try to develop in yourself over the years? How does Meg demonstrate these qualities?
- **Narrative Piece**—Thinking about what has happened so far, retell the last few scenes in the story with Meg going under IT's control instead of Charles Wallace.

_____

_____

_____

_____

_____

_____

_____

_____

_____

_____

_____

_____

_____

_____

Name _____

Date _____

Close Reading the Literature

Directions: Closely reread the end of chapter 9. Start with the line where Meg remembers that "Mrs Whatsit had said, 'Meg, I give you your faults.'" Stop at the end of the chapter. Read each question, and then revisit the text to find the evidence that supports your answer.

1. What text evidence helps the reader predict how Meg's faults will help her fight against IT?

   _____

   _____

   _____

2. In what ways does Meg try to fight against IT?

   _____

   _____

3. Why do Mr. Murry and Calvin decide to tesser with Meg and leave Charles Wallace alone on Camazotz?

   _____

   _____

   _____

4. Based on the events in the story, what do you expect to happen after they leave Camazotz?

   _____

   _____

   _____

Name _____

Date _____

Making Connections–Character Dialogue

Throughout this section, there is a lot of dialogue among the characters. Using carefully chosen vocabulary, diverse sentence structure, and proper grammar when writing dialogue can make a huge difference in how someone reads text.

Read the following text adapted from *A Wrinkle in Time*.

> "Charles. Charles Wallace," said Mr. Murry.
>
> "What do you want?" Charles Wallace asked.
>
> "I'm your father, Charles. Look at me," said Mr. Murry.
>
> "Hi, Father," said Charles Wallace.
>
> "That isn't Charles Wallace," said Meg. "Charles isn't like that. IT has him."

Now, read this text quoted directly from Madeleine L'Engle's text:

> Mr. Murry released Meg and knelt in front of the little boy. "Charles," his voice was tender. "Charles Wallace."
>
> "What do you want?"
>
> "I'm your father, Charles. Look at me."
>
> The pale blue eyes seemed to focus on Mr. Murry's face. "Hi, Pop," came an insolent voice.
>
> "That isn't Charles!" Meg cried. "Oh, Father, Charles isn't like that. IT has him."

Directions: Now, it's your turn to write some dialogue. Choose two characters from the book. You can choose anyone! On another sheet of paper, write a short conversation between the characters. The characters need to discuss how they feel about leaving Charles Wallace on Camazotz. Be sure to go back at least once to edit your conversation for vocabulary, sentence structure, and grammar.

Name _____

Date _____

Creating with the Story Elements

Directions: Thinking about the story elements of character, setting, and plot in a novel is very important to understanding what is happening and why. Complete **one** of the following activities about what you've read so far. Be creative and have fun!

Characters

Create a T-chart that contrasts Charles Wallace when he arrives on Camazotz to when he is under IT's control. The chart should have many descriptive terms for Charles Wallace's actions and personality.

Setting

Rewrite the scene in which Meg finds her father, but place it in a different setting. Instead of being stuck on Camazotz, place the characters in a happier, safer setting. Meg and Charles Wallace have just found and saved their father. How might their reunion differ from the one in the book? Be creative and unique when you write the dialogue among the characters. Also, include in your scene how the characters will get home.

Plot

Draw a picture of the most important scene in this section. Include all of the key characters in the scene and add labels to make sure that it is clear what is happening in the scene.

Teacher Plans—Section 5
Chapters 10–12

Vocabulary Overview

Ten key words from this section are provided below with definitions and sentences about how the words are used in the book. Choose one of the vocabulary activity sheets (pages 55 or 56) for students to complete as they read this section. Monitor students as they work to ensure the definitions they have found are accurate and relate to the text. Finally, discuss these important vocabulary words with students. If you think these words or other words in the section warrant more time devoted to them, there are suggestions in the introduction for other vocabulary activities (page 5).

Word	Definition	Descriptive Sentence
atrophied (ch. 10)	made smaller because of illness	Parts of IT are **atrophied** from lack of use, so the Murrys and Calvin are able to resist its power.
fallibility (ch. 10)	the likelihood of making an error	Meg realizes that her father has human **fallibility** and he can't always keep her safe and secure.
assuaged (ch. 10)	to make something go away	Aunt Beast immediately **assuages** Meg's pain.
acute (ch. 11)	sharp, severe	Meg has **acute** pain after she tessers through the Black Thing with her father.
despondency (ch. 11)	feeling hopeless and sad	While discussing how to help Charles Wallace, Meg has a wave of **despondency** come over her.
reproving (ch. 11)	expressing disappointment in a corrective way	Aunt Beast has to speak in a **reproving** way to get Meg to see that she is hurting her father.
formidably (ch. 12)	inspiring fear and respect	Mrs Which's voice rolls **formidably** across a group when she speaks to them.
indignation (ch. 12)	anger at something that is unfair	Meg gets angry at Calvin and hopes that her **indignation** will keep her fear from showing to everyone.
permeating (ch. 12)	spreading throughout	The pulse of IT is **permeating** throughout the room as Meg tries to save Charles Wallace.
vestige (ch. 12)	description of something that has just disappeared or is about to disappear	Meg uses her last **vestige** of consciousness to save herself from IT's control.

Understanding Vocabulary Words

Directions: The following words are in this section of the book. Use context clues and reference materials to determine an accurate definition for each word.

Word	Definition
atrophied (ch. 10)	
fallibility (ch. 10)	
assuaged (ch. 10)	
acute (ch. 11)	
despondency (ch. 11)	
reproving (ch. 11)	
formidably (ch. 12)	
indignation (ch. 12)	
permeating (ch. 12)	
vestige (ch. 12)	

Name _____

Date _____

During-Reading Vocabulary Activity

Directions: As you read these chapters, choose five important words from the story. Use these words to complete the word flow chart below. On each arrow, write a word. In each box, explain how the connected pair of words relates to each other. An example for the words *acute* and *assuage* has been done for you.

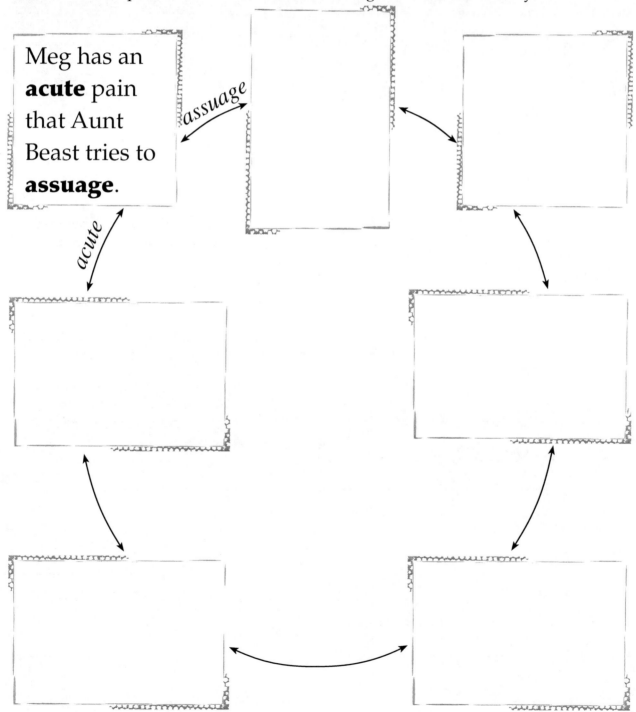

Meg has an **acute** pain that Aunt Beast tries to **assuage**.

Analyzing the Literature

Provided below are discussion questions you can use in small groups, with the whole class, or for written assignments. Each question is given at two levels so you can choose the right question for each group of students. Activity sheets with these questions are provided (pages 58–59) if you want students to write their responses. For each question, a few key discussion points are provided for your reference.

Story Element	■ Level 1	▲ Level 2	Key Discussion Points
Character	What different issues does Meg blame Calvin and her father for when she first wakes up from tessering?	Why is Meg so angry when she first wakes up from tessering?	Meg is very angry because they left Charles Wallace on Camazotz. She blames Calvin for telling her father to leave. She blames her father for not being strong enough to keep them safe.
Character	Describe Aunt Beast.	What is the importance of the short role that Aunt Beast plays in Meg's experiences?	Aunt Beast protects and cares for Meg in a way that no other character has in the book. Even Meg's mother doesn't handle her so carefully. Although strong, Meg needs someone to take care of her at this particular time in the story. Meg grows stronger simply because of Aunt Beast's unconditional love for her.
Plot	Why does Meg have to go back to Camazotz alone to rescue Charles Wallace from IT?	Describe the reasons that Meg comes to realize that she alone can rescue Charles Wallace from IT.	Meg decides to go back to Camazotz before she fully understands why she is the only one who can save Charles Wallace. The Mrs Ws have made it clear that they cannot step in to help. They can only guide her. It is not until she gets back to Camazotz that she realizes her ability to love and be loved is what makes her the only one who can save her brother. Not everyone has that strength of character.
Plot	Where do you think the three Mrs Ws are taking the children at the end of the book?	Predict what problem the Murry children will have to tackle next.	As long as students have reasons for their predictions, accept any response.

Name _____

Date _____

Analyzing the Literature

Directions: Think about the section you have just read. Read each question and state your response with textual evidence.

1. What different issues does Meg blame Calvin and her father for when she first wakes up from tessering?

_____

_____

_____

_____

2. Describe Aunt Beast.

_____

_____

_____

3. Why does Meg have to go back to Camazotz alone to rescue Charles Wallace from IT?

_____

_____

_____

_____

4. Where do you think the three Mrs Ws are taking the children at the end of the book?

_____

_____

_____

_____

▲ Analyzing the Literature

Directions: Think about the section you have just read. Read each question and state your response with textual evidence.

1. Why is Meg so angry when she first wakes up from tessering?

   _____

   _____

   _____

   _____

2. What is the importance of the short role that Aunt Beast plays in Meg's experiences?

   _____

   _____

   _____

   _____

3. Describe the reasons that Meg comes to realize that she alone can rescue Charles Wallace from IT.

   _____

   _____

   _____

   _____

4. Predict what problem the Murry children will have to tackle next.

   _____

   _____

   _____

Name _____

Date _____

Reader Response

Directions: Choose one of the following prompts about this section to answer. Be sure you include a topic sentence in your response, use textual evidence to support your opinion, and provide a strong conclusion that summarizes your opinion.

Writing Prompts

- **Narrative Piece**—Choose one of the main characters in the book and describe why you would or would not like to be friends with that character.
- **Informative/Explanatory Piece**—Describe how the author uses character dialogue to move the story along in the last chapter.

_____

_____

_____

_____

_____

_____

_____

_____

_____

_____

_____

_____

_____

_____

Name _____

Date _____

Chapters 10–12

Close Reading the Literature

Directions: Closely reread the section where Meg saves Charles Wallace from IT in chapter 12. Start with where she passes CENTRAL Central Intelligence, "Her steps got slower and slower as she passed the great bronzed doors . . ." Stop reading when they land on the ground together and Charles Wallace cries out, "Meg! Oh, Meg!" Read each question, and then revisit the text to find the evidence that supports your answer.

1. What text helps the reader understand how Meg is feeling as she approaches IT's dome?

   _____

   _____

   _____

2. Use text evidence to explain how anger affects IT's control of Meg.

   _____

   _____

   _____

3. How does Meg come to realize that she possesses something that IT doesn't have?

   _____

   _____

   _____

   _____

4. Use the book to tell why love is the most powerful tool for Meg in her challenge to save Charles Wallace.

   _____

   _____

   _____

   _____

© Shell Education

#40217—Instructional Guide: A Wrinkle in Time

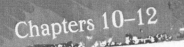

Name _____

Date _____

Making Connections—IT, the Brain

One of the antagonists in this novel is IT. Strangely enough, IT is actually a huge brain. The rhythm produced by IT controls everyone and everything on the planet of Camazotz.

Directions: Find out more information about these five parts of the brain: **cerebrum**, **cerebellum**, **brain stem**, **pituitary gland**, and **hypothalamus**. Research them in resource books or online. On another sheet of paper, explain the function of each. Finally, label at least these five parts of the brain on this diagram.

These websites might help you:

- http://kidshealth.org/kid/htbw/brain.html
- http://www.sciencekids.co.nz/sciencefacts/humanbody/brain.html

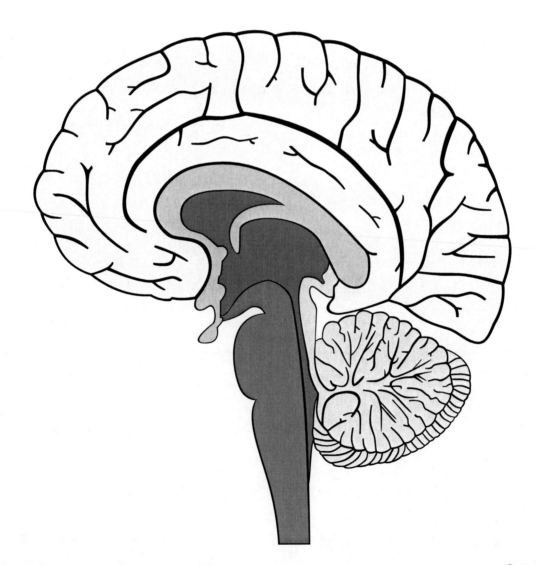

Name _____

Date _____

Creating with the Story Elements

Directions: Thinking about the story elements of character, setting, and plot in a novel is very important to understanding what is happening and why. Complete **one** of the following activities about what you've read so far. Be creative and have fun!

Characters

Draw the final scene in the book. Your image should show the Murry family reuniting as the Mrs Ws show up to take the children on another adventure.

Setting

Create a diagram that shows all of the planets visited in this novel. Draw lines to indicate the tesseracts that were taken between the planets.

- Earth
- Uriel
- the 2D planet
- the Happy Medium's planet
- Camazotz
- Ixchel

Plot

Draw a comic strip version of the climactic scene in which Meg takes on IT to save Charles Wallace. However, in this version, put yourself in Meg's shoes. Through the comic strip, tell how your personality strengths might have been able to overcome IT and save Charles Wallace. Be creative. You can exaggerate your personal traits to make yourself more superhero like.

Name _____

Date _____

Post-Reading Theme Thoughts

Directions: Read each of the statements in the first column. Choose a main character from *A Wrinkle in Time*. Think about that character's point of view. From that character's perspective, decide if the character would agree or disagree with the statements. Record the character's opinion by marking an X in Agree or Disagree for each statement. Explain your choices in the third column using text evidence.

Character I Chose: _____

Statement	Agree	Disagree	Explain Your Answer
Good should always win over evil.			
Your physical appearance is not very important in society.			
Love is stronger than hatred.			
Individual differences are crucial to a society.			

Name _____

Date _____

Culminating Activity: Understanding the "Bad Guy"

Overview: In most works of fiction, there is an antagonist. This is the character who causes trouble for the protagonist, or the "good guy." The antagonist, then, is the "bad guy." In *A Wrinkle in Time*, the Black Thing is the primary antagonist. The Black Thing is a force of evil that wants to control others. If you have read much fantasy fiction, you know that a force of darkness is a common antagonist.

Directions: Think of some books you have read and movies you have seen. Consider the characters who are the dark forces working against the heroes. In what way are those characters like the Black Thing in *A Wrinkle in Time*? Select one dark-force antagonist and make a Venn diagram, comparing and contrasting it with the Black Thing.

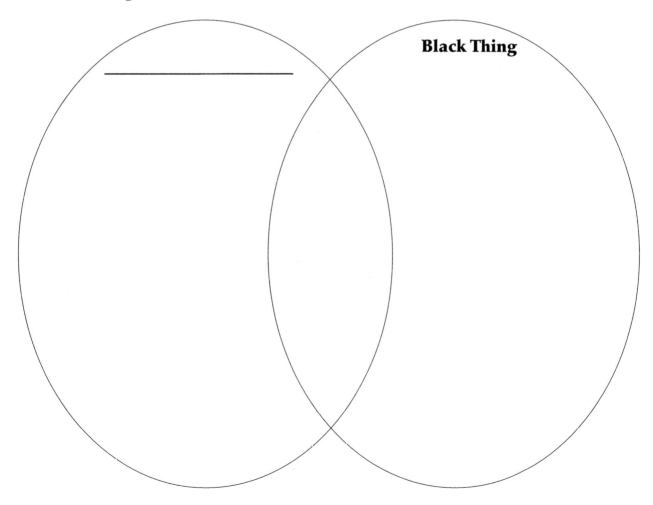

Black Thing

Name _____

Date _____

Culminating Activity: Understanding the "Bad Guy" (cont.)

Directions: When your Venn diagram is complete and you have a good understanding of the Black Thing, select one of the culminating projects below to complete:

Write a scene from a movie in which the Black Thing meets the dark-force character from another book or movie. What do they say to each other? What happens? The scene should be at least two pages in length. It should be true to the nature of each character.

Make a movie poster for *A Wrinkle in Time* that shows the ominous threat of the Black Thing. The viewer should be able to get a good understanding of the Black Thing's nature just by your depiction.

Imagine that the Black Thing takes shape. Create a three-dimensional model of the Black Thing as you envision it. You may use any medium, including clay, papier-mâché, and more.

Name _____

Date _____

Comprehension Assessment

Directions: Circle the letter for the best response to each question.

1. What is the meaning of the word *tesseract* as it is used in the book?

    a. a three-dimensional cube

    b. a wrinkle in a piece of string

    c. a wrinkling of time and space

    d. jumping back in history

2. Which detail from the book best supports your answer to question 1?

    a. "Speaking of ways, pet, by the way, there is such a thing as a tesseract."

    b. "What *is* a tesseract?"

    c. "We travel in the fifth dimension. This is something you can understand, Meg."

    d. "You add that to the other four dimensions and you can travel through space without having to go the long way around."

3. Write the main idea of the text below in the graphic organizer.

    "Wee wwill cconnttinnue tto ffightt!" . . .

    "And we're not alone, you know, children," came Mrs Whatsit, the comforter. "All through the universe it's being fought, all through the cosmos, and my, but it's a grand and exciting battle . . . . You think about that, and maybe it won't seem strange to you that some of our very best fighters have come right from your own planet, and it's a little planet, dears, out on the edge of a little galaxy. You can be proud that it's done so well."

Main Idea (question 3)

Details (question 4)

Details (question 4)

Comprehension Assessment (cont.)

4. Choose two details that support the main idea from question 3. Add them to the graphic organizer in question 3.

   a. Light will help defeat the Black Thing.

   b. Evil will win in the end.

   c. Earth is helping in the battle against the Black Thing.

   d. The Mrs Ws have been alive a long time.

5. Which statement best expresses one of the themes of the book?

   a. Try to fit in with others.

   b. Love conquers evil.

   c. Always work together to reach a goal.

   d. It is hard to tesser.

6. What detail from the book provides the best evidence for your answer to number 5?

   a. "Love. That was what she had that IT did not have."

   b. "I don't know if they're really like everybody else, or if they're able to pretend they are."

   c. "No! *Alike* and *equal* are not the same thing at all!"

   d. "Poor thing," Mrs Whatsit said, "we've worn her out. It's very hard work for her."

7. What is the purpose of this sentence from the book?
   "I do not know everything; still many things I understand."

   _____

   _____

   _____

8. Which other quotation from the story serves a similar purpose?

   a. "We can't take any credit for our talents. It's how we use them that counts."

   b. "People are more than just the way they look."

   c. "Don't try to comprehend with your mind. Your minds are very limited. Use your intuition."

   d. "You see, though we travel together, we travel alone."

Response to Literature:
The Symbolism Behind Camazotz

Overview: *A Wrinkle in Time* was published in 1962. That year in history is marked by many things of importance, perhaps the most significant of which were the Civil Rights Movement in the United States and the Cold War between the United States and the Union of Soviet Socialist Republics (U.S.S.R.).

The Civil Rights Movement was based on the belief that all people are created equal. That means they should be given equal rights of citizenship under the law. Many people fought against laws that were unfair for African Americans. Some people even died for this cause.

The Cold War was a long standoff between the U.S.S.R. with its communism and the fight for democracy in the United States. Some people in the United States thought that the "Soviet threat" could end American freedoms. No physical battles were fought like in World War II. However, it was a very scary time as weapons were used to threaten each side.

Directions: Select either of these times in history and explain how Camazotz and the events of *A Wrinkle in Time* can be seen as a commentary on the real history. What do you think the author might be saying about the real history through the symbolism of what happens in the book? What might Camazotz and the activity of IT represent? Write a researched opinion essay that shows your understanding of the real-world history. Use historic facts and examples, and also cite the novel to support your thinking. In conclusion, explain what the author may be saying about the real event.

Your essay response to literature should follow these guidelines:

- **State a clear opinion.**
- **Be at least 750 words in length.**
- **Cite at least three real events in history.**
- **Cite at least three references from the novel.**
- **Provide a conclusion that summarizes your thoughts and findings.**

Final essays are due on _____.

Name _____

Date _____

Response to Literature Rubric

Directions: Use this rubric to evaluate student responses to how *A Wrinkle in Time* is a reflection of the history of the time period when it was published.

	Exceptional Writing ☐	Quality Writing ☐	Developing Writing ☐
Focus and Organization	States a clear opinion and elaborates well. Engages the reader from hook through the middle to the conclusion. Demonstrates clear understanding of the intended audience and purpose of the piece.	Provides a clear and consistent opinion. Maintains a clear perspective and supports it through elaborating details. Makes the opinion clear in the opening hook and summarizes well in the conclusion.	Provides an inconsistent point of view. Does not support the topic adequately or misses pertinent information. Provides lack of clarity in the beginning, middle, and conclusion.
Text Evidence	Provides comprehensive and accurate support. Includes relevant and worthwhile text references.	Provides limited support. Provides few supporting text references.	Provides very limited support for the text. Provides no supporting text references.
Written Expression	Uses descriptive and precise language with clarity and intention. Maintains a consistent voice and uses an appropriate tone that supports meaning. Uses multiple sentence types and transitions well between ideas.	Uses a broad vocabulary. Maintains a consistent voice and supports a tone and feelings through language. Varies sentence length and word choices.	Uses a limited and unvaried vocabulary. Provides an inconsistent or weak voice and tone. Provides little to no variation in sentence type and length.
Language Conventions	Capitalizes, punctuates, and spells accurately. Demonstrates complete thoughts within sentences, with accurate subject-verb agreement. Uses paragraphs appropriately and with clear purpose.	Capitalizes, punctuates, and spells accurately. Demonstrates complete thoughts within sentences and appropriate grammar. Paragraphs are properly divided and supported.	Incorrectly capitalizes, punctuates, and spells. Uses fragmented or run-on sentences. Utilizes poor grammar overall. Paragraphs are poorly divided and developed.

The responses provided here are just examples of what students may answer. Many accurate responses are possible for the questions throughout this unit.

During-Reading Vocabulary Activity—Section 1:
Chapters 1–3 (page 16)
1. The word **sullen** describes Meg Murry's character because at the beginning of the book, she is often gloomy and moody. This is especially true when thinking about how she behaves at school.
2. Charles Wallace seems **prodigious** in a couple of ways. He is so smart that he seems to read the minds of his closest family members. He did not speak until he was four, but he skipped all the toddler talk, and now he speaks like a young adult.

Close Reading the Literature—Section 1:
Chapters 1–3 (page 21)
1. The Murrys are surprised during Mrs Whatsit's visit because she is such a strange character. Meg is thrown off guard by her arrival and by her prior relationship with Charles Wallace. Mrs. Murry is surprised when Mrs Whatsit uses the word *tesseract* on her departure.
2. Charles Wallace is "small and vulnerable" sitting in the kitchen during the storm. He makes his mother and sister sandwiches in the middle of the night. That shows that he is helpful and kind.
3. Meg is very frustrated by Mrs Whatsit's visit in the middle of the night. She thinks, "I'll bet she is the tramp. I'll bet she did steal those sheets." Clearly she doesn't think very highly of the woman on first appearance in their house.
4. Mrs Whatsit has a strong relationship with Charles Wallace already. The fact that she knows about tesseracts makes it seem like maybe she will help Meg and Charles Wallace find their father.

Making Connections—Section 1:
Chapters 1–3 (page 22)

This experiment is based on the activity on http://candleandsoap.about.com/od/soapmaking basics/ss/howsoapcleans.htm. You can see pictures of each step as well as an explanation on that site.

1. In the jar with just oil and water, the two liquids separate. Water is denser than oil, so it will be on the bottom of the jar. In the jar with soap added, the soap keeps the oil and water from separating for a few minutes. If you leave the jar sitting out, you will see that over time, the liquids separate again.
2. The reactions in the two jars are different because the soap surrounds the oil molecules and keeps the oil from joining together again. When cleaning, this allows the oil and/or dirt to be washed away.

During-Reading Vocabulary Activity—Section 2:
Chapters 4–5 (page 26)
1. Describing a tesseract is **ineffable** because it is not easy to do. There is no straightforward answer that can be stated. To explain tesseracts you have to use examples and mathematical terms.

2. Mrs Whatsit's true **corporeal** state might look like anything. Students can describe any form based on what they have read so far. They need to support their answers with what they've read.

Close Reading the Literature—Section 2:
Chapters 4–5 (page 31)
1. Meg feels very strange the first time she travels by "wrinkling" through time. She feels "completely alone." She feels like her body has separated from her mind. It takes a bit of time for her legs and arms to tingle and come back to her. She even thinks, "Here there was nothing to feel."
2. Calvin seems to understand more than Meg does. He is also a lot bigger than Meg, so it must take him longer to reappear after tessering.
3. The characters in this scene are very protective of each other. As soon as she can hear, Meg hears Charles Wallace calling for Calvin and her. "'Meg!' he shouted. 'Calvin! Where are you?'" She answers him as soon as she can. Then, Calvin starts right away by threatening, "If you've hurt Meg, any of you—." These immediate reactions make it clear that the characters are very concerned about each other.
4. Students need to use evidence from this close reading section to answer this question. As long as they support their predictions, any answer is acceptable.

Making Connections—Section 2:
Chapters 4–5 (page 32)
6. Students should think of how to make it seem like Meg is jumping through time.

Close Reading the Literature—Section 3:
Chapters 6–7 (page 41)
1. Charles Wallace has a different reaction to the food than Calvin and Meg. Calvin and Meg think that the food is delicious. Charles Wallace thinks the food "tastes like sand." He is able to shut his mind to the man with red eyes completely. Meg and Calvin are being partially hypnotized by the man with red eyes.
2. The man with red eyes wants Charles Wallace to open his mind and allow the man to control him. Charles Wallace thinks that he can go into the man's mind and still leave when he wants to.
3. Charles Wallace believes that he has to try to trust the man with red eyes because he thinks it is the only way to find his father and continue the fight against the Black Thing. "It's the Black Thing. We have to do what Mrs Which sent us to do." Throughout the book, Charles Wallace has always understood things on a higher level than Meg and Calvin.
4. At the end of the section, Meg shrieks, "That isn't Charles! Charles is gone!" She means that his mind is gone. His body may be there, but his mind is no longer his own. The man with red eyes is controlling his mind. So, in essence, Charles Wallace is gone.

During-Reading Vocabulary Activity—Section 4: Chapters 8–9 (page 46)

1. The leaders of Camazotz do not allow the people of their planet to **deviate** from each other. If people do things differently, the leaders punish them very firmly.

2. CENTRAL Central Intelligence is an **ominous** building because it is large and overpowering when you approach it. Also, when you enter it, the serious nature of everyone inside leads you to know that it is a very frightening, serious place.

Close Reading the Literature—Section 4: Chapters 8–9 (page 51)

1. Meg's faults will help her fight against IT because she is stubborn. She thinks of her faults as "Anger, impatience, stubbornness." When you are stubborn, you do not like to do what others tell you to do. This will help Meg because IT is trying to control everything she does and says. She will get angry and stubborn, so she will be able to fight against IT's power.

2. Meg tries to fight against IT by reciting a nursery rhyme. That does not work, so she switches to the Declaration of Independence. She begins to recite the Periodic Table of Elements. When that becomes too rhythmic, she switches to difficult mathematics problems.

3. Mr. Murry and Calvin decide to tesser with Meg and leave Charles Wallace alone on Camazotz because IT is too powerful. Meg is about to fall under IT's spell when the three characters tesser.

4. Students should predict that the characters will find a way to save Charles Wallace. They may mention that the Mrs Ws will help or that Meg will find the strength to return on her own.

Close Reading the Literature—Section 5: Chapters 10–12 (page 61)

1. As Meg approaches IT's dome, she is feeling afraid. Her body tries to slow down the trip, but she still gets to IT. "No matter how slowly her feet had taken her at the end, they had taken her there."

2. Anger affects IT's control of Meg by drawing her closer to IT. At first, she thinks that anger will save her, but quickly she realizes that IT thrives on her anger.

3. When Charles Wallace says that Mrs Whatsit hates Meg, she realizes how wrong he is. That is when she knows that she has love, and IT could never have love.

4. Love is the most powerful tool for Meg in her challenge to save Charles Wallace because others love her and she loves them. She loves Charles Wallace even when he is controlled by IT. By loving him, she overpowers IT's hatred and pulls the real Charles Wallace back to her.

Making Connections—Section 5: Chapters 10–12 (page 62)

The functions of these parts of the brain are as follows:

- The cerebrum controls thinking and your voluntary muscles.
- The cerebellum controls balance and movement.
- The brain stem controls breathing, digesting, and blood circulation.
- The pituitary gland controls growth.
- The hypothalamus controls your body temperature.

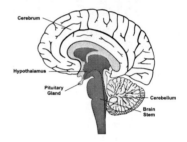

Comprehension Assessment (pages 67-68)

1. c. a wrinkling of time and space

2. d. "You add that to the other four dimensions and you can travel through space without having to go the long way around."

3. Main Idea: The Black Thing is being fought.

4. Supporting Details: a. Light will help defeat the Black Thing; c. Earth is helping in the battle against the Black Thing.

5. b. Love conquers evil.

6. a. "Love. That was what she had that IT did not have."

7. Just because you don't understand something doesn't mean you should stop trying. Often, if you think about it hard enough, you'll be able to infer what it means.

8. c. "Don't try to comprehend with your mind. Your minds are very limited. Use your intuition."